W9-AGB-885

This library edition published in 2012 by Walter Foster Publishing, Inc.
Distributed by Black Rabbit Books.
P.O. Box 3263 Mankato, Minnesota 56002

Designed and published by Walter Foster Publishing, Inc.
Walter Foster is a registered trademark.

Copyright © 2006 Disney Enterprises, Inc./Pixar. Disney/Pixar elements © Disney/Pixar; Hudson Hornet is a trademark of DaimlerChrysler; Volkswagen trademarks, design patents, and copyrights are used with the approval of the owner, Volkswagen AG; Model T is a registered trademark of Ford Motor Company; Fiat is a trademark of Fiat S.p.A.; Chevrolet Impala is a trademark of General Motors; Porsche is a trademark of Porsche; Jeep is a registered trademark of DaimlerChrysler; Mercury is a registered trademark of Ford Motor Company; Plymouth Superbird is a trademark of DaimlerChrysler; Ferrari elements are trademarks of Ferrari S.p.A.; Sarge's rank insignia design used with the approval of the U.S. Army. Petty marks used by permission of Petty Marketing LLC; inspired by the Cadillac Range by Ant Farm (Lord, Michels, and Marquez) © 1974.

No license is herein granted for the use of any drawing of a Pixar character for any commercial purpose, including but not limited to, the placing of any such drawing on an article of merchandise or the reproduction, public display, or sale of any such drawing. Any use other than home use by the reader of any such drawing is prohibited.

Printed in Mankato, Minnesota, USA by CG Book Printers, a division of Corporate Graphics.

First Library Edition

Library of Congress Cataloging-in-Publication Data

Learn to draw Disney Pixar Cars : draw your favorite characters, step by simple step / illustrated by the Disney Storybook Artists ; inspired by the character designs created by Pixar Animation Studios. -- 1st library ed.
    p. cm. -- (Learn to draw ; dc22l)
  ISBN 978-1-936309-32-0 (hardcover)
  1. Cartoon characters--Juvenile literature. 2. Drawing--Technique--Juvenile literature. 3. Cars (Motion picture)--Juvenile literature. I. Disney Storybook Artists. II. Pixar (Firm) III. Title: Disney Pixar cars.
  NC1764.8.M67L43 2011
  741.5'1--dc22

2011008878

042011
17320

9 8 7 6 5 4 3 2 1

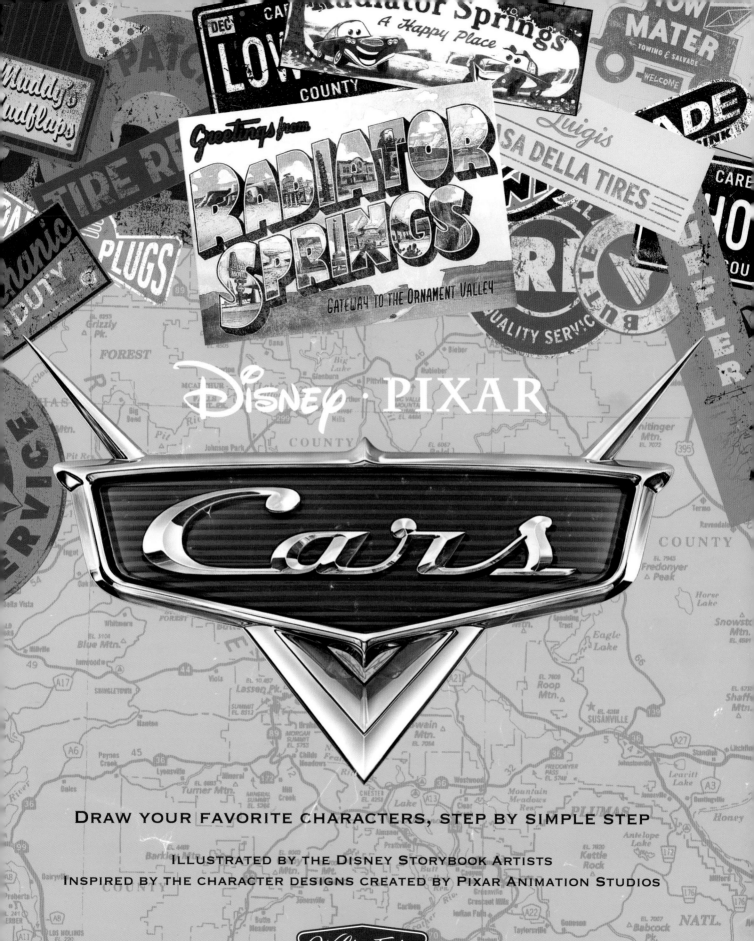

Disney · PIXAR

Cars

DRAW YOUR FAVORITE CHARACTERS, STEP BY SIMPLE STEP

ILLUSTRATED BY THE DISNEY STORYBOOK ARTISTS
INSPIRED BY THE CHARACTER DESIGNS CREATED BY PIXAR ANIMATION STUDIOS

Walter Foster®

WALTER FOSTER PUBLISHING, INC.
3 WRIGLEY, SUITE A
IRVINE, CA 92618
WWW.WALTERFOSTER.COM

It's time for the biggest car race of the year, the Dinoco 400. In this world, cars are the characters, and rookie sensation Lightning McQueen rolls out of his trailer to swarming reporters and cheering fans.

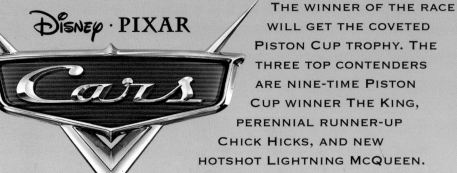

The winner of the race will get the coveted Piston Cup trophy. The three top contenders are nine-time Piston Cup winner The King, perennial runner-up Chick Hicks, and new hotshot Lightning McQueen. And with The King retiring, his lucrative Dinoco sponsorship is also up for grabs.

McQueen takes the lead! But at his pit stop, he refuses to change tires to save time. It's a bad move. In the final lap, his rear tires blow! Chick and The King catch up, and the race is too close to call!

While they wait for the results, The King tells McQueen he needs to treat his pit crew better, but McQueen isn't listening. He's daydreaming about his future glory . . . until he learns the race was a three-way tie! A tie-breaker race will be held in California in one week.

Reluctantly McQueen makes a quick appearance for Rusteze, his current sponsor. Then he

He tears up the asphalt street and ends up hanging between two telephone poles.

The next morning, McQueen wakes up in the town impound. The Sheriff orders the friendly, rusty tow truck named Mater to tow McQueen to traffic court.

In court, Sally, the town's attorney, argues that the ruined road will turn away desperately needed customers. Doc, the judge, sentences McQueen to stay until he fixes the road.

McQueen is hooked to the messy paver named Bessie. After an hour he says he's finished, but the road looks terrible. Doc challenges McQueen to a race. If McQueen wins, he can go. But if McQueen loses, he will have to stay and finish the road Doc's way.

When the race begins, McQueen leaves Doc in the dust, speeding ahead and ripping around a turn . . . right over the edge of a deep ditch and into a cactus patch.

backs into his trailer and hits the road with his driver, Mack. McQueen pushes Mack to drive through the night. He wants to be the first to reach the California race. After many long hours, Mack dozes off. He swerves and McQueen falls out of the trailer!

Terrified, McQueen dodges the oncoming traffic and desperately follows Mack down an off-ramp—only to find it isn't Mack he was following! Lost and panicked, McQueen speeds through the small town of Radiator Springs. The Sheriff takes chase, making backfire noises that sound like gunshots, causing McQueen to drive wildly.

3

THAT NIGHT MCQUEEN GOES BACK TO WORK. BY MORNING, THERE IS A BEAUTIFUL, NEWLY PAVED STRETCH OF ROAD.

DOC FINDS MCQUEEN BACK AT THE DIRT TRACK TRYING TO GET THE TURN HE MISSED. HE TELLS MCQUEEN THAT IF HE RACES ON DIRT AND WANTS TO TURN LEFT, SOMETIMES HE SHOULD STEER RIGHT. MCQUEEN LAUGHS AT THE ADVICE, BUT WHEN NO ONE IS WATCHING HE TRIES IT . . . AND FALLS RIGHT INTO THE CACTUS PATCH AGAIN.

THE TOWNSFOLK ARE INSPIRED BY THE NEW STRETCH OF ROAD, SO THEY BEGIN FIXING UP THEIR SHOPS. THAT NIGHT, MATER TAKES MCQUEEN TRACTOR TIPPING. AND MCQUEEN IS HAVING FUN UNTIL A COMBINE CHASES THEM OFF!

BACK IN TOWN, SALLY OVERHEARS MCQUEEN EXPLAINING THAT WINNING THE PISTON CUP MEANS HE'LL HAVE FAME, FORTUNE, AND A BIG NEW SPONSOR. HE EVEN PROMISES MATER A HELICOPTER RIDE. THRILLED, MATER DECLARES MCQUEEN HIS BEST FRIEND.

LATER SALLY APPROACHES MCQUEEN AND ASKS IF HE INTENDS TO KEEP HIS PROMISE TO MATER. FOLKS IN RADIATOR SPRINGS TRUST ONE ANOTHER, AND SHE DOESN'T WANT MATER TO GET HURT.

THE NEXT MORNING, MATER AWAKENS THE WHOLE TOWN TO SHOW THEM THAT THE ROAD IS FINISHED. THEN MCQUEEN GOES SHOPPING—AND HE BECOMES THE BEST CUSTOMER RADIATOR SPRINGS HAS SEEN IN A LONG TIME.

THE NEXT MORNING, MCQUEEN WANDERS INTO DOC'S BACK OFFICE, WHERE HE FINDS THREE PISTON CUPS AND REALIZES THAT DOC IS THE FABULOUS HUDSON HORNET! DOC IS FURIOUS THAT MCQUEEN HAS DISCOVERED HIS SECRET AND HE ANGRILY SHOOS AWAY MCQUEEN.

SALLY INVITES MCQUEEN ON A DRIVE UP THE MOUNTAIN. AT THE TOP, SALLY TELLS THE STORY OF HOW SHE LEFT LOS ANGELES AND FOUND HER HOME IN RADIATOR SPRINGS. SHE ALSO EXPLAINS HOW RADIATOR SPRINGS WAS BYPASSED WHEN THE INTERSTATE WAS BUILT. SHE'D GIVE ANYTHING TO HAVE SEEN IT IN ITS HEYDAY.

LATER, MCQUEEN SECRETLY WATCHES DOC GRACEFULLY RACING AT THE DIRT TRACK. WHEN DOC DISCOVERS MCQUEEN, HE LEAVES—BUT MCQUEEN FOLLOWS HIM. DOC FINALLY LETS OUT HIS SECRET: WHEN HE RETURNED TO THE RACING WORLD AFTER RECOVERING FROM A BIG WRECK, DOC WAS REPLACED BY A ROOKIE LIKE MCQUEEN.

THE NEXT MORNING, MATER AWAKENS THE WHOLE TOWN TO SHOW THEM THAT THE ROAD IS FINISHED. THEN MCQUEEN GOES SHOPPING—AND HE BECOMES THE BEST CUSTOMER RADIATOR SPRINGS HAS SEEN IN A LONG TIME.

SALLY IS TOUCHED THAT MCQUEEN HELPED ALL THE TOWNSFOLK. AS DUSK SETTLES, MCQUEEN CUES THE TOWNSFOLK TO TURN ON THEIR NEWLY REPAIRED NEON LIGHTS. RADIATOR SPRINGS IS JUST LIKE IT WAS IN ITS HEYDAY. EVERYONE CRUISES HAPPILY.

BUT THE MOOD IS CRUSHED BY AN INVASION OF REPORTERS. MCQUEEN HAS BEEN FOUND! MACK ARRIVES TO TAKE MCQUEEN TO THE BIG RACE. MCQUEEN FINDS SALLY IN THE CROWD. SPEECHLESS, HE LISTENS TO HER AS SHE WISHES HIM LUCK. THEN HE SADLY DRIVES INTO THE TRAILER AND LEAVES.

THE TIE-BREAKER RACE IS SET TO BEGIN. INSIDE HIS TRAILER, MCQUEEN TRIES TO PREPARE, BUT HIS HEART ISN'T IN IT. AS THE RACE BEGINS, MCQUEEN FALLS FAR BEHIND . . . UNTIL HE REALIZES ALL HIS PALS FROM RADIATOR SPRINGS HAVE COME TO BE HIS PIT CREW!

NEWLY DETERMINED, MCQUEEN CATCHES UP WITH THE LEADERS. HIS PIT CREW TAKES CARE OF HIM, FIXING A BLOWN TIRE. AND WHEN CHICK BUMPS INTO HIM, HE QUICKLY RECOVERS BY USING THE DIRT-TURN TRICK DOC TAUGHT HIM. SOON HE PULLS INTO FIRST PLACE!

WHEN CHICK CAUSES THE KING TO CRASH BEHIND HIM, MCQUEEN HEARS THE CROWD GASP AND LOOKS UP AT THE STADIUM SCREEN. THE IMAGE REMINDS HIM OF DOC'S CRASH. MCQUEEN SLAMS ON HIS BRAKES JUST BEFORE THE FINISH LINE.

CHICK WINS THE RACE BUT NO ONE CARES. MCQUEEN REVERSES AND PUSHES THE KING TO A SECOND-PLACE FINISH AND THE CROWD GOES WILD.

MCQUEEN IS OFFERED THE DINOCO SPONSOR-SHIP! BUT MCQUEEN DECIDES TO STAY WITH THE LOYAL GUYS FROM RUST-EZE. HE DOES ASK DINOCO FOR ONE SMALL FAVOR, THOUGH: A HELICOPTER RIDE FOR HIS FRIEND MATER.

ALONE ON THE MOUNTAIN, SALLY LOOKS OUT OVER THE VALLEY WHEN MCQUEEN SURPRISES HER. HE SAYS HE'S OPENING UP HIS HEADQUARTERS IN TOWN. THEIR ROMANTIC MOMENT IS INTERRUPTED AS MATER APPEARS IN THE HELICOPTER, SINGING. SALLY LAUGHS AND TEARS OFF DOWN THE MOUNTAIN. MCQUEEN CHASES HER. THERE'S NOWHERE ELSE HE'D RATHER BE.

GETTING STARTED

READY, SET, GO! THAT'S RIGHT, YOU'RE OFF AND READY TO DRAW, COLOR, AND PAINT YOUR WAY TO CREATING REVVED-UP CARS. THOUGH MCQUEEN MAY REQUIRE SOME FANCY TOOLS FOR A TUNE-UP, ALL YOU NEED ARE A FEW SIMPLE SUPPLIES TO DRAW THIS RACE CAR AND ALL HIS PALS. A GRAPHITE PENCIL WILL GET YOUR DRAWING ENGINE RUNNING. THEN YOU CAN SPICE UP THINGS RAMONE-STYLE BY MOVING ON TO COLOR WITH FELT-TIP MARKERS, COLORED PENCILS, WATERCOLORS, OR ACRYLIC PAINTS. BE SURE TO USE THE TIPS IN THIS BOOK TO KEEP THESE CARS IN PRIME CONDITION. READY TO ROLL? *KA-CHOW!*

colored pencils

drawing pencil

sharpener

eraser

markers

paint brush and paints

JUST FOLLOW THE SIMPLE STEPS!

STEP 1

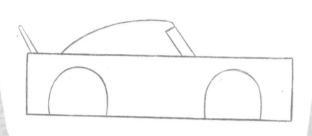

FIRST DRAW THE BASIC SHAPES.

STEP 2

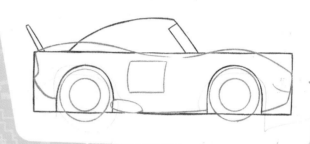

EACH NEW STEP IS SHOWN IN BLUE.

STEP 3

SIMPLY FOLLOW THE BLUE LINES TO
ADD THE DETAILS.

STEP 4

NOW DARKEN THE LINES YOU WANT TO KEEP
AND ERASE THE REST.

FINALLY USE CRAYONS, MARKERS, COLORED PENCILS,
OR PAINTS TO ADD COLOR TO YOUR DRAWING.

LIGHTNING MCQUEEN

McQueen is a hotshot rookie race car who cares only about two things: winning and the fame and fortune that come with it. But all that changes when he suddenly finds himself in the sleepy old town of Radiator Springs.

STEP 1

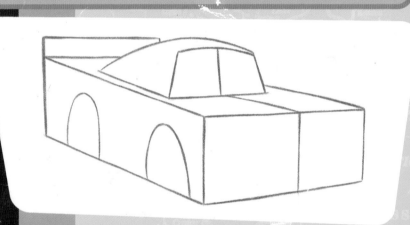

don't make pupils too big

NO!

YES!

STEP 2

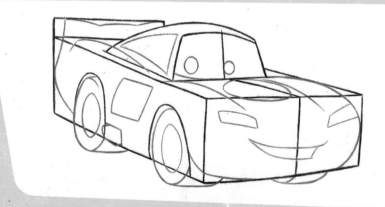

NITROADE
HI-ENERGY DRINK

STEP 3

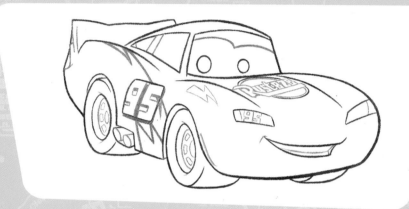

you can give McQueen different expressions by adjusting his eyelids

sad

curious

intense

when McQueen looks down, don't bury eyes into body

NO!

YES!

STEP 4

MATER

PARKY'S SPARK PLU

MATER IS A FRIENDLY, ENTHUSIASTIC TOW TRUCK WITH A BIG HEART, WHO IS ALWAYS WILLING TO GIVE A HELPING HAND. HE IS THE SELF-PROCLAIMED WORLD'S BEST BACKWARDS DRIVER, AND HE ALSO GETS A KICK OUT OF TRACTOR TIPPING.

STEP 1

YES!
mirrors are at irregular angles

NO!
mirrors are not perfectly aligned

STEP 2

STEP 3

keep facial expressions off center to emphasize Mater's goofiness

YES!   YES!

NO!
too centered

STEP 4

YES!   NO!

his misshapen buckteeth aren't perfect squares—and there's a gap between them

11

SALLY

SALLY, A SMART AND BEAUTIFUL SPORTS CAR, IS DETERMINED TO RESTORE RADIATOR SPRINGS TO THE BUSTLING TOWN IT WAS IN ITS HEYDAY. ORIGINALLY AN ATTORNEY FROM LOS ANGELES, SHE SHOWS McQUEEN THAT SOMETIMES IT'S GOOD TO LIVE LIFE IN THE SLOW LANE.

STEP 1

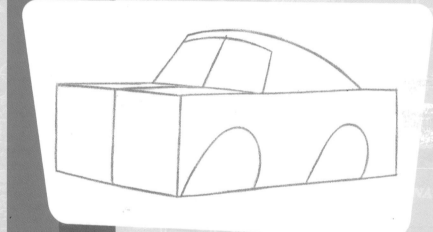

Sally's eyebrows are heaviest at the peaks

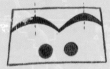

YES!

NO!

STEP 2

STEP 3

Sally is just about a tire width
smaller than McQueen

  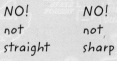

YES!
spokes
have
curved
pattern

NO!
not
straight

NO!
not
sharp

STEP 4

13

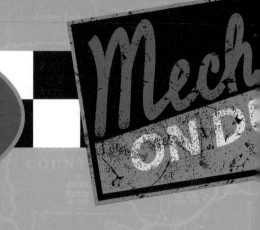

DOC HUDSON

DOC IS A RESPECTED AND ADMIRED TOWN DOCTOR, AND HE'S THE JUDGE IN RADIATOR SPRINGS. BUT HE HAS A MYSTERIOUS PAST. PROTECTIVE OF THE TOWN, DOC CHERISHES THE QUIET AND SIMPLE LIFE. HE WANTS NOTHING TO DO WITH THE FLASHY RACE CAR McQUEEN.

STEP 1

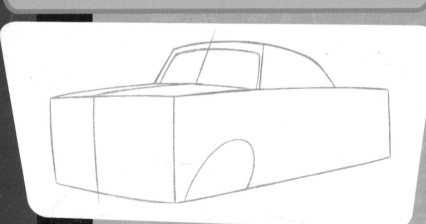

NO!

YES!

centerline helps transform Doc's windshield into glasses

STEP 2

STEP 3

Doc's grille is like a rainbow built over the central letter A

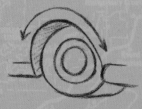

NO!
front fender isn't round

STEP 4

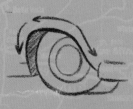

YES!
fender curves into front bumper

15

SHERIFF

SHERIFF IS THE KEEPER OF THE PEACE IN RADIATOR SPRINGS, AND HE TAKES HIS JOB VERY SERIOUSLY. HE ENJOYS TELLING STORIES ABOUT HIS BELOVED MOTHER ROAD, AND HE ESPECIALLY LOVES TAKING NAPS BEHIND THE RADIATOR SPRINGS BILLBOARD.

STEP 1

Sheriff's rounded, heavy body is shaped like a cream-filled donut

STEP 2

STEP 3

Sheriff's grille resembles a big, bushy mustache

STEP 4

Sheriff's big, red light is shaped like a dome

17

RED

Despite being a big, strong fire engine, Red is very shy and sensitive. If he's not cheerfully helping out his neighbors, you can find him lovingly tending to his flower garden.

STEP 1

YES!

NO!

eyelids show Red is shy—not aggressive

STEP 2

The Top Down TRUCKSTOP CONVERTIBLE WAITRESSES

STEP 3

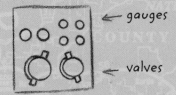

← gauges

← valves

 valves can turn

STEP 4

front   back

Red's wheel curves out from front tire but is hidden within rear tires

RAMONE

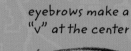

RAMONE LOVES TO CRUISE LOW AND SLOW—AND TO LOOK GOOD DOING IT. THE OWNER OF THE LOCAL CUSTOM PAINT AND BODY SHOP, RAMONE IS A PAINT ARTIST EXTRAORDINAIRE. HE ENJOYS TRYING ON COOL NEW LOOKS BY RE-PAINTING HIMSELF ALMOST EVERY DAY.

STEP 1

eyebrows make a "V" at the center

YES!

NO!

STEP 2

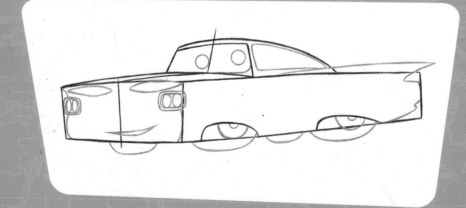

STEP 3

keep flames interesting and
varied—not too uniform

YES!

NO!

STEP 4

21

FLO

Flo is a sassy, no-nonsense show car with a big heart. Married to Ramone, she runs the local diner, where she serves the "finest fuel in 50 states."

STEP 1

NO! don't make tailfins too high

YES! top of fins are level with top of cab

STEP 2

STEP 3

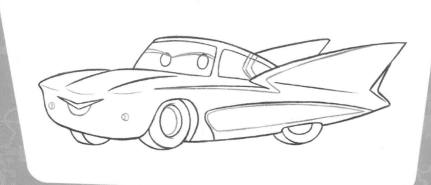

YES!   NO!

Flo's eyelashes connect
like windshield wipers
and have thick peaks

STEP 4

YES!   NO!

NO!

top lip is long and
thin—bottom lip is
shorter and fatter

23

LUIGI AND GUIDO

LUIGI IS AN EXUBERANT ITALIAN SPORTS CAR WHO RUNS THE LOCAL TIRE SHOP. HIS BEST FRIEND AND ASSISTANT IS AN ITALIAN FORKLIFT NAMED GUIDO. BOTH ARE AVID RACE FANS WHO DREAM OF PERFORMING A REAL PIT STOP.

STEP 1

NO!

not hard edges

YES!

edges are rounded

STEP 2

STEP 1

STEP 2

YES! head is wider at base

NO! head is not square

FILLMORE AND SARGE

FILLMORE IS A BELIEVER IN ALL THINGS NATURAL. HIS "NATURALLY" MESSY YARD DRIVES HIS NEIGHBOR SARGE, A PATRIOTIC VETERAN, ABSOLUTELY NUTS. DESPITE THEIR CONSTANT BICKERING, THEY CAN'T LIVE WITHOUT EACH OTHER.

STEP 1

STEP 2

YES!

wheels close together and angle inward

NO!

wheels not far apart and evenly aligned

STEP 1

YES!

NO!

eyebrows more like window shades than windshield wipers

eyebrows don't curve

STEP 2

YES!

NO!

tires have tread

tires aren't slick like racing tires

27

THE KING

THE KING IS A RACING LEGEND WHO HAS WON MORE
PISTON CUPS THAN ANY OTHER CAR IN HISTORY.
BUT HE MANAGES TO KEEP HIS PRIORITIES STRAIGHT.
HE KNOWS THAT IT TAKES MORE THAN TROPHIES TO
BE A TRUE CHAMPION.

STEP 1

spoiler is same height
as distance from the
trunk to ground

STEP 2

STEP 3

NO! The King's front hood is pointed, not rounded

STEP 4

CHICK

RE-VOI REBUILT ALT

CHICK IS A RACING VETERAN WITH A CHIP ON HIS SHOULDER. HE'S A RUTHLESS COMPETITOR WHO IS NOTORIOUS FOR CHEATING HIS WAY TO SECOND PLACE. ALWAYS A RUNNER-UP, HE'LL DO ANYTHING TO WIN.

STEP 1

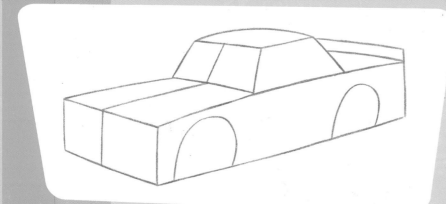

YES!

tires are big and wide

NO!

not too thin

STEP 2

STEP 3

YES!

NO!

Chick has beady pupils and a sharp peak between his eyes

STEP 4

Chick considers himself prime real estate and is covered with sponsor stickers—so get creative with sticker shapes and placement

31

FRIENDSHIP—KA-CHOW!

Once a superstar rookie without a friend, McQueen learned a lot about friendship by living in the slow lane in Radiator Springs. Friendship comes in all shapes, sizes, and colors—from Red, the fire truck, and Guido, the tiny forklift, to beautiful blue Sally and the rusty beloved Mater. As you create your art, remember your friends and their characteristics too. Sometimes it helps to draw from your heart—something McQueen can confirm as being part of the joy of slowing down to enjoy life . . . and friends.